THE DESERT DRUM

Robert Hichens

[ZHINGOORA BOOKS]

This edition is published by
Zhingoora Books.

Contents

I

I am not naturally superstitious. The Saharaman is. He has many strange beliefs. When one is at close quarters with him, sees him day by day in his home, the great desert, listens to his dramatic tales of desert lights, visions, sounds, one's common-sense is apt to be shaken on its throne. Perhaps it is the influence of the solitude and the wide spaces, of those far horizons of the Sahara where the blue deepens along the edge of the world, that turns even a European mind to an Eastern credulity. Who can tell? The truth is that in the Sahara one can believe what one cannot believe in London. And sometimes circumstances—chance if you like to call it so—steps in, and seems to say, "Your belief is well founded."

Of all the desert superstitions the one which appealed most to my imagination was the superstition of the desert drum. The Sahara-man declares that far away from the abodes of men and desert cities, among the everlasting sand dunes, the sharp beating, or dull, distant rolling of a drum sometimes breaks upon the ears of travellers voyaging through the desolation.

They look around, they stare across the flats, they see nothing. But the mysterious music continues. Then, if they be Sahara-bred, they commend themselves to Allah, for they know that some terrible disaster is at hand, that one of them at least is doomed to die.

Often had I heard stories of the catastrophes which were immediately preceded by the beating of the desert drum. One night in the Sahara I was a witness to one which I have never been able to forget.

On an evening of spring, accompanied by a young Arab and a negro, I rode slowly down a low hill of the Sahara, and saw in the sandy cup at my feet the tiny collection of hovels called Sidi-Massarli. I had been in the saddle since dawn, riding over desolate tracks in the heart of the desert. I was hungry, tired, and felt almost like a man hypnotised. The strong air, the clear sky, the everlasting flats devoid of vegetation, empty of humanity, the monotonous motion of my slowly cantering horse—all these things combined to dull my brain and to throw me into a peculiar condition akin to the condition of a man in a trance. At Sidi-Massarli I was to pass the night. I drew rein and looked down on it with lacklustre eyes.

I saw a small group of palm-trees, guarded by a low wall of baked brown earth, in which were embedded many white bones of dead camels. Bleached, grinning heads of camels hung from more than one of the trees, with strings of red pepper and round stones. Beyond the wall of this palm garden, at whose foot was a furrow full of stagnant brownish-yellow water, lay a handful of wretched earthen hovels, with flat roofs of palmwood and low wooden doors. To be exact, I think there were five of them. The Bordj, or Travellers' House, at which I was to be accommodated for the night, stood alone near a tiny source at the edge of a large sand dune, and was a small, earth-coloured building with a pink tiled roof, minute arched windows, and an open stable for the horses and mules. All round the desert rose in humps of sand, melting into stony ground where the saltpetre lay like snow on a wintry world. There were but few signs of life in this place; some stockings drying on the wall of a ruined Arab café, some kids frisking by a heap of sacks, a few pigeons circling about a low square watch-tower, a black donkey brooding on a dust heap. There were some signs of death; carcasses of camels stretched here and there in frantic and fantastic postures, some bleached and smooth, others red and horribly odorous.

The wind blew round this hospitable township of the Sahara, and the yellow light of evening began to glow above it. It seemed to me at that moment the dreariest place in the dreariest dream man had ever had.

Suddenly my horse neighed loudly. Beyond the village, on the opposite hill, a white Arab charger caracoled, a red cloak gleamed. Another traveller was coming in to his night's rest, and he was a Spahi. I could almost fancy I heard the jingle of his spurs and accoutrements, the creaking of his tall red boots against his high peaked saddle. As he rode down towards the Bordj—by this time, I, too, was on my way—I saw that a long cord hung from his saddle-bow, and that at the end of this cord was a man, trotting heavily in the heavy sand like a creature dogged and weary. We came in to Sidi-Massarli simultaneously, and pulled up at the same moment before the arched door of the Bordj, from which glided a one-eyed swarthy Arab, staring fixedly at me. This was the official keeper of the house. In one hand he held the huge door key, and as I swung myself heavily on the ground I heard him, in Arabic, asking my Arab attendant, D'oud, who I was and where I hailed from.

But such attention as I had to bestow on anything just then was given to the Spahi and his companion. The Spahi was a magnificent man, tall, lithe, bronze-brown and muscular. He looked about thirty-four, and had the face of a desert eagle. His piercing black eyes stared me calmly out of countenance, and he sat on his spirited horse like a statue, waiting patiently till the guardian of the Bordj was ready to attend to him. My gaze travelled from him along the cord to the man at its end, and rested there with pity. He, too, was a fine specimen of humanity, a giant, nobly built, with a superbly handsome face, something like that of an undefaced Sphinx. Broad brows sheltered his enormous eyes. His rather thick lips were parted to allow his panting breath to escape, and his dark, almost black skin, was covered with sweat. Drops of sweat coursed down his bare arms and his mighty chest, from which his ragged burnous was drawn partially away. He was evidently of mixed Arab and negro parentage. As he stood by the Spain's horse, gasping, his face expressed nothing but physical exhaustion. His eyes were bent on the sand, and his arms hung down loosely at his sides. While I looked at him the Spahi suddenly gave a tug at the cord to which he was attached. He moved in nearer to the horse, glanced up at me, held out his hand, and said in a low, musical voice, speaking Arabic:

"Give me a cigarette, Sidi."

I opened my case and gave him one, at the same time diplomatically handing another to the Spahi. Thus we opened our night's acquaintance, an acquaintance which I shall not easily forget.

In the desolation of the Sahara a travelling intimacy is quickly formed. The one-eyed Arab led our horses to the stable, and while my two attendants were inside unpacking the tinned food and the wine I carried with me on a mule, I entered into conversation with the Spahi, who spoke French fairly well. He told me that he was on the way to El Arba, a long journey through the desert from Sidi-Massarli, and that his business was to convey there the man at the end of the cord.

"But what is he? A prisoner?" I asked.

"A murderer, monsieur," the Spahi replied calmly.

I looked again at the man, who was wiping the sweat from his face with one huge hand. He smiled and made a gesture of assent.

"Does he understand French?"

"A little."

"And he committed murder?"

"At Tunis. He was a butcher there. He cut a man's throat."

"Why?"

"I don't know, monsieur. Perhaps he was jealous. It is hot in Tunis in the summer. That was five years ago, and ever since he has been in prison."

"And why are you taking him to El Arba?"

"He came from there. He is released, but he is not allowed to live any more in Tunis. Ah, monsieur, he is mad at going, for he loves a dancing-girl, Aïchouch, who dances with the Jewesses in the café by the lake. He wanted even to stay in prison, if only he might remain in Tunis. He never saw her, but he was in the same town, you understand. That was something. All the first day he ran behind my horse cursing me for taking him away. But now the sand has got into his throat. He is so tired that he can scarcely run. So he does not curse any more."

The captive giant smiled at me again. Despite his great stature, his powerful and impressive features, he looked, I thought, very gentle and submissive. The story of his passion for Aïchouch, his desire to be near her, even in a prison cell, had appealed to me. I pitied him sincerely.

"What is his name?" I asked.

"M'hammed Bouaziz. Mine is Said."

I was weary with riding and wanted to stretch my legs, and see what was to be seen of Sidi-Massarli ere evening quite closed in, so at this point I lit a cigar and prepared to stroll off.

"Monsieur is going for a walk?" asked the Spahi, fixing his eyes on my cigar.

"Yes."

"I will accompany monsieur."

"Or monsieur's cigar-case," I thought.

"But that poor fellow," I said, pointing to the murderer. "He is tired out."

"That doesn't matter. He will come with us."

The Spahi jerked the cord and we set out, the murderer creeping over the sand behind us like some exhausted animal.

By this time twilight was falling over the Sahara, a grim twilight, cold and grey. The wind was rising. In the night it blew half a gale, but at this hour there was only a strong breeze in which minute sand-grains danced. The murderer's feet were shod with patched slippers, and the sound of these slippers shuffling close behind me made me feel faintly uneasy. The Spahi stared at my cigar so persistently that I was obliged to offer him one. When I had done so, and he had loftily accepted it, I half turned towards the murderer. The Spahi scowled ferociously. I put my cigar-case back into my pocket. It is unwise to offend the powerful if your sympathy lies with the powerless.

Sidi-Massarli was soon explored. It contained a Café Maure, into which I peered. In the coffee niche the embers glowed. One or two ragged Arabs sat hunched upon the earthen divans playing a game of cards. At least I should have my coffee after my tinned dinner. I was turning to go back to the Bordj when the extreme desolation of the desert around, now fading in the shadows of a moonless night, stirred me to a desire. Sidi-Massarli was dreary enough. Still it contained habitations, men. I wished to feel the blank, wild emptiness of this world, so far from the world of civilisation from which I had come, to feel it with intensity. I resolved to mount the low hill down which I had seen the Spahi ride, to descend into the fold of desert beyond it, to pause there a moment, out of sight of the hamlet, listen to the breeze, look at the darkening sky, feel the sand-grains stinging my cheeks, shake hands with the Sahara.

But I wanted to shake hands quite alone. I therefore suggested to the Spahi that he should remain in the Café Maure and drink a cup of coffee at my expense.

"And where is monsieur going?"

"Only over that hill for a moment."

"I will accompany monsieur."

"But you must be tired. A cup of——"

"I will accompany monsieur."

In Arab fashion he was establishing a claim upon me. On the morrow, when I was about to depart, he would point out that he had guided me round Sidi-

Massarli, had guarded me in my dangerous expedition beyond its fascinations, despite his weariness and hunger. I knew how useless it is to contend with these polite and persistent rascals, so I said no more.

In a few minutes the Spahi, the murderer and I stood in the fold of the sand dunes, and Sidi-Massarli was blotted from our sight.

II

The desolation here was complete. All around us lay the dunes, monstrous as still leviathans. Here and there, between their strange, suggestive shapes, under the dark sky one could see the ghastly whiteness of the saltpetre in the arid plains beyond, where the low bushes bent in the chilly breeze. I thought of London—only a few days' journey from me— revelled for a moment in my situation, which, contrary to my expectation, was rather emphasised by the presence of my companions. The gorgeous

Spahi, with his scarlet cloak and hood, his musket and sword, his high red leggings, the ragged, sweating captive in his patched burnous, ex-butcher looking, despite his cord emblem of bondage, like reigning Emperor—they were appropriate figures in this desert place. I had just thought this, and was regarding my Sackville Street suit with disgust, when a low, distinct and near sound suddenly rose from behind a sand dune on my left. It was exactly like the dull beating of a tom-tom. The silence preceding it had been intense, for the breeze was as yet too light to make more than the faintest sighing music, and in the gathering darkness this abrupt and gloomy noise produced, I supposed, by some hidden nomad, made a very unpleasant, even sinister impression upon me. Instinctively I put my hand on the revolver which was slung at my side in a pouch of gazelle skin. As I did so, I saw the Spahi turn sharply and gaze in the direction of the sound, lifting one hand to his ear.

The low thunder of the instrument, beaten rhythmically and persistently, grew louder and was evidently drawing nearer. The musician must be climbing up the far side of the dune. I had swung round to face him, and expected every moment to see some wild figure appear upon the summit, defining itself against the cold and gloomy sky. But none came. Nevertheless, the noise increased till it was a roar, drew near till it was actually upon us. It seemed to me that I heard the sticks striking the hard, stretched skin furiously, as if some phantom drummer were stealthily encircling us, catching us in a net, a trap of horrible, vicious uproar. Instinctively I threw a questioning, perhaps an appealing, glance at my two companions. The Spahi had dropped his hand from his ear. He stood upright, as if at attention on the parade-ground of Biskra. His face was set— afterwards I told myself it was fatalistic. The murderer, on the other hand, was smiling. I remember the gleam of his big white teeth. Why was he smiling? While I asked myself the question the roar of the tom-tom grew gradually less, as if the man beating it were walking rapidly away from us in the direction of Sidi-Massarli. None of us said a word till only a faint, heavy throbbing, like the beating of a heart, I fancied, was audible in the darkness. Then I spoke, as silence fell.

"Who is it?"

"Monsieur, it is no one."

The Spain's voice was dry and soft.

"What is it?"

"Monsieur, it is the desert drum. There will be death in Sidi-Massarli to-night."

I felt myself turn cold. He spoke with such conviction. The murderer was still smiling, and I noticed that the tired look had left him. He stood in an alert attitude, and the sweat had dried on his broad forehead.

"The desert drum?" I repeated.

"Monsieur has not heard of it?"

"Yes, I have heard—but—it can't be. There must have been someone."

I looked at the white teeth of the murderer, white as the saltpetre which makes winter in the desert.

"I must get back to the Bordj," I said abruptly.

"I will accompany monsieur."

The old formula, and this time the voice which spoke it sounded natural. We went forward together. I walked very fast. I wanted to catch up that music, to prove to myself that it was produced by human fists and sticks upon an instrument which, however barbarous, had been fashioned by human hands. But we entered Sidi-Massarli in a silence, only broken by the soughing of the wind and the heavy shuffle of the murderer's feet upon the sand.

Outside the Café Maure D'oud was standing with the white hood of his burnous drawn forward over his head; one or two ragged Arabs stood with him.

"They've been playing tom-toms in the village, D'oud?"

"Monsieur asks if——"

"Tom-toms. Can't you understand?"

"Ah! Monsieur is laughing. Tom-toms here! And dancers, too, perhaps! Monsieur thinks there are dancers? Fatma and Khadija and Aïchouch————"

I glanced quickly at the murderer as D'oud mentioned the last name, a name common to many dancers of the East. I think I expected to see upon his face some tremendous expression, a revelation of the soul of the man who had run for one whole day through the sand behind the Spahi's horse, cursing at the end of the cord which dragged him onward from Tunis.

But I only met the gentle smile of eyes so tender, so submissive, that they were as the eyes of a woman who had always been a slave, while the ragged Arabs laughed at the idea of tom-toms in Sidi-Massarli.

When we reached the Bordj I found that it contained only one good-sized room, quite bare, with stone floor and white walls. Here, upon a deal table, was set forth my repast; the foods I had brought with me, and a red Arab soup served in a gigantic bowl of palmwood. A candle guttered in the glass neck of a bottle, and upon the floor were already spread my gaudy striped quilt, my pillow, and my blanket. The Spahi surveyed these preparations with a deliberate greediness, lingering in the narrow doorway.

I sat down on a bench before the table. My attendants were to eat at the Café Maure.

"Where are you going to sleep?" I asked of D'oud.

"At the Café Maure, monsieur, if monsieur is not afraid to sleep alone. Here is the key. Monsieur can lock himself in. The door is strong."

I was helping myself to the soup. The rising wind blew up the skirts of the Spahi's scarlet robe. In the wind—was it imagination?—I seemed to hear some thin, passing echoes of a tom-tom's beat.

"Come in," I said to the Spahi. "You shall sup with me to-night, and—and you shall sleep here with me."

D'oud's expressive face became sinister. Arabs are almost as jealous as they are vain.

"But, monsieur, he will sleep in the Café Maure. If monsieur wishes for a companion, I——"

"Come in," I repeated to the Spahi. "You can sleep here to-night."

The Spahi stepped over the lintel with a jingling of spurs, a rattling of accoutrements. The murderer stepped in softly after him, drawn by the cord. D'oud began to look as grim as death. He made a ferocious gesture towards the murderer.

"And that man? Monsieur wishes to sleep in the same room with him?"

I heard the sound of the tom-tom above the wail of the wind.

"Yes," I said.

Why did I wish it? I hardly know. I had no fear for, no desire to protect myself. But I remembered the smile I had seen, the Spahi's saying, "There will be death in Sidi-Massarli to-night," and I was resolved that the three men who had heard the desert drum together should not be parted till the morning. D'oud said no more. He waited upon me with his usual diligence, but I could see that he was furiously angry. The Spahi ate ravenously. So did the murderer, who more than once, however, seemed to be dropping to sleep over his food. He was apparently dead tired. As the wind was now become very violent I did not feel disposed to stir out again, and I ordered D'oud to bring us three cups of coffee to the Bordj. He cast a vicious look at the Spahi and went out into the darkness. I saw him no more that night. A boy from the Café Maure brought us coffee, cleared the remains of our supper from the table, and presently muttered some Arab salutation, departed, and was lost in the wind.

The murderer was now frankly asleep with his head upon the table, and the Spahi began to blink. I, too, felt very tired, but I had something still to say. Speaking softly, I said to the Spahi:

"That sound we heard to-night——"

"Monsieur?"

"Have you ever heard it before?"

"Never, monsieur. But my brother heard it just before he had a stroke of the sun. He fell dead before his captain beside the wall of Sada. He was a tirailleur."

"And you think this sound means that death is near?

"I know it, monsieur. All desert people know it. I was born at Touggourt, and how should I not know?"

"But then one of us——"

I looked from him to the sleeping murderer.

"There will be death in Sidi-Massarli tonight, monsieur. It is the will of Allah. Blessed be Allah."

I got up, locked the heavy door of the Bordj, and put the key in the inner pocket of my coat. As I did so, I fancied I saw the heavy black lids of the murderer's closed eyes flutter for a moment. But I cannot be sure. My head was aching with fatigue. The Spahi, too, looked stupid with sleep. He jerked the cord, the murderer awoke with a start, glanced heavily round, stood up. Pulling him as one would an obstinate dog, the Spahi made him lie down on the bare floor in the corner of the Bordj, ere he himself curled up in the thick quilt which had been rolled up behind his high saddle. I made no protest, but when the Spahi was asleep, his lean brown hand laid upon his sword, his musket under his shaven head, I pushed one of my blankets over to the murderer, who lay looking like a heap of rags against the white wall. He smiled at me gently, as he had smiled when the desert drum was beating, and drew the blanket over his mighty limbs and face.

I did not mean to sleep that night. Tired though I was my brain was so excited that I felt I should not. I blew out the candle without even the thought that it would be necessary to struggle against sleep. And in the darkness I heard for an instant the roar of the wind outside, the heavy breathing of my two strange companions within. For an instant—then it seemed as if a shutter was drawn suddenly over the light in my brain. Blackness filled the room where the thoughts develop, crowd, stir in endless activities. Slumber fell upon me like a great stone that strikes a man down to dumbness, to unconsciousness.

Far in the night I had a dream. I cannot recall it accurately now. I could not recall it even the next morning when I awoke. But in this dream, it seemed to me that fingers felt softly about my heart. I was conscious of their fluttering touch. It was as if I were dead, and as if the doctor laid for a moment his hand upon my heart to convince himself that the pulse of life no longer beat. And this action wove itself naturally into the dream I had. The fingers so soft, so surreptitious, were lifted from my breast, and I sank deeper into the gulf of sleep, below the place of dreams. For I was a tired man that night. At the first breath of dawn I stirred and woke. It was cold. I put out one hand and drew up my quilt. Then I lay still. The wind had sunk. I no longer heard it roaring over the desert. For a moment I hardly remembered where I was, then memory came back and I listened for the deep breathing of the Spahi and the murderer. Even when the wind blew I had heard it. I did not hear it now. I lay there under my quilt for some minutes listening. The silence was intense. Had they gone already, started on their way to El Arba? The Bordj was in darkness, for the windows were very small, and dawn had scarcely begun to break outside and had not yet filtered in through the wooden shutters which barred them. I disliked this complete silence, and felt about for the matches I had laid beside the candle before turning in. I could not find them. Someone had moved them, then. The heaviness of sleep had quite left me now, and I remembered clearly all the incidents of the previous evening. The roll of the desert drum sounded again in my ears. I threw off my quilt, got up, and moved softly over the stone floor towards the corner where the murderer had lain down to sleep. I bent down to touch him and touched the stone. They had gone, then! It was strange that I had not been waked by their departure. Besides, I had the key of the door. I thrust my hand into the breast-pocket of my coat which I had worn while I slept. The key was no longer there. Then I remembered my dream and the fingers fluttering round my heart. Stumbling in the blackness I came to the place where the Spahi had lain, stretched out my hands and felt naked flesh. My hands recoiled from it, for it was very cold.

Half-an-hour later the one-eyed Arab who kept the Bordj, roused by my beating upon the door with the butt end of my revolver, came with D'oud to ask what was the matter. The door had to be broken in. This took some time. Long before I could escape, the light of the sun, entering through the little arched windows, had illumined the nude corpse of the Spahi, the gaping red wound in his throat, the heap of murderer's rags that lay across his feet.

M'hammed Bouaziz, in the red cloak, the red boots, sword at his side, musket slung over his shoulder, was galloping over the desert on his way to freedom.

But six months later he was taken at night outside a café by the lake at Tunis. He was gazing through the doorway at a girl who was posturing to the sound of pipes between two rows of Arabs. The light from the café fell upon his face, the dancer uttered a cry.

"M'hammed Bouaziz!"

"Aïchouch!"

The law avenged the Spahi, and this time it was not to prison they led my friend of Sidi-Massarli, but to an open space before a squad of soldiers just when the dawn was breaking.

End of the book.

www.ingramcontent.com/pod-product-compliance
Lightning Source LLC
Chambersburg PA
CBHW071350310526
45790CB00018B/1404